WISDOM

OF

AHKENATEN AS I AM

by

Francis E. Revels-Bey

Photo of statue of Ahkenaten

Pen & Ink Drawing (black ink on white paper) of
Ahkenaten by author, Francis E. Revels-Bey, after a
deep two hour meditation on 7/4/2017.

First Edition - First paperback printing.
Printed in the United States of America
ISBN: 978-1-7286-0204-2

Table of Contents

Contact Information

Brother Francis' Offerings

About Brother Francis E. Revels-Bey

Dedication

I, Brother Francis E. Revels-Bey, fully dedicate this book and its entire contents to the being known as **Ahkenaten**, who is considered to be the one who started monotheism and held Aten the disk in high esteem and understood Its purpose. He has come and gone in numerous lives as Sananda, Serapis Bey and Quan Yin which others have said.

Ahkenaten, thank you for your Patience, Compassion and Golden White Light. Thank you for your Divine Grace and being my Blue Beacon Light.

Spiritual Message from The Angel of Grace

"Welcome Beloveds as you have arrived in The Temple of Grace within its Heart Chamber. Here you gather collectively and individually with all of your being to remember your Divine Nature of Grace as Ahkenaten taught these divine principles as maxims in his great mystery school during his reign. As you know he taught many men and women this to prepare them for the Divine Feminine and Divine Masculine to be activated deeply into the Souls of every being upon the matrix called Gaia. He left his fingerprint upon the codified plates in the Great Central Sun and beyond".

1

"Ahkenaten seeded himself long ago into **Amenaten** and many others during his life time and taught everyone how to be in more than one life stream and realm at will. Amenaten is the author and keeper of this material and much of what you shall read here is exactly what Amenaten was given to teach throughout his numerous life streams. If we placed all of his adepts' knowledge together it would wrap around the matrix called Gaia a million times. There are no more secrets even though many are ritualistically trying to hide them. This MAterial is designed to be flowing and glowing like a star-seed."

"Just know that your entire journey is a never ending
process where you continue to unfold
so that you shall grow in awareness
to keep remembering that you are an infinite
self-realized truth."

The Author's Remembrance

Ahkenaten came to me first in 2003 and again once in 2006, but I wasn't sure who he was and most of my energy from the mid-1990's through 2008 was focused on researching my mom's side of the family who had Cherokee and Irish blood and my dad's side had Blackfoot bloodlines mixed as well. One day in 2009 my Sister Vernell pointed out to me that she had a photo of Ahkenaten's mother and how she favors my late Mother Grace in appearance by face and eyes. Once I saw the picture I could see the resemblance as well.

He kept "popping in and out" and sometimes I would see this very large head in the ceiling of my bedroom in the middle of the night. However, it never occurred to me to ask someone. I am forever grateful that Ahkenaten kept coming into my dreams and while I was awake he began to make his presence known to me. His energy kept growing around me in 2009 so much that I would start to meditate on him. Then, in 2010 while I was giving information out during a live streaming online broadcast for one of my weekly shows called *"Decree & It Shall Be"* he comes and his I AM Presence was enormous to say the least as his aura could be felt throughout the premises that special evening. During that particular show I was teaching "The Art & Science of Prayers, Affirmations, Meditations and Decrees" and he roared in with a gentle fun-loving sort of communication that left me with many pearls and gems of wisdom.

As I channeled my late Mother Grace, her mother - Grandma Charlotte, The Angel of Grace and many Ascended Masters, Ahkenaten would arrive and eventually, I knew the difference between him and every other soul's presence. *He would always project The Great Central Sun's energy*. Ahkenaten caused me to reflect back to the time when I began to channel my **Creative Pathwork Meditations** on a regular basis in 1996 when I lived on Long Island in NY.

I was receiving meditations within 12 hours before my evening group meditations I was conducting weekly on Long Island and in New Jersey. *Finally, in the year 2000, I channeled CPM-067 entitled "The Great Central Sun" and in 2001 CPM-071 entitled "Remembrance - Reawakening Your Divinity."* The more I meditated and grew deeper in my awareness, I realized that there was something special happening here. During the period of 2010 into 2012, I began to feel him reach into me so much. I began to feel like I had to really listen when I sensed he was near. So one day after a long private meditation I heard him address me as **Amenaten.** After much research and constant meditation the meaning of the name came into my heart through him...He would say to me: *"I call you Amenaten, because your prayers are effectual whenever you pray for other people."* I would feel a sense of joy whenever I playfully hummed and sang his name with him responding: *"Whose that knocking at my door? Ahkenaten. Whose that ringing my bell? Ahkenaten. It's Ahkenaten and he is ringing my bell."* Finally, I contacted a spiritual colleague around August 3, 2015 and asked could she give me one of her angel readings. I wanted to get insight from someone else about Ahkenaten and she revealed that she channels him as well. The day she chose was August 11, 2015. It was my late Mother Grace's birthday, but I didn't reveal that to her until after the reading. It was revealed that I worked closely with Ahkenaten during the time he was a Pharaoh and how he had adopted me in his own way. He taught me within his palace then his temple in Akhetaten. I experienced many journeys with him into the heart of The Great Central Sun from that moment several times a week. Eventually, I begin to realize my love of Crystals, energy work similar to Tai Chi and long periods of being alone along with many soul travels gave my remembrance rich meanings. I realized how Mother Grace, Grandma Charlotte, Serapis Bey, Sananda, Saint Germain and The Angel of Grace were leading me toward him. Ever since then I felt this to be a real spiritual connection the clearer his spiritual transmissions became for me. All the things I teach come through my association with him. Now he says to share his wisdom and I am as I AM.

"Welcome to The Wisdom of Ahkenaten as I AM"

Brother Francis E. Revels-Bey as Amenaten

A Universal Decree as I AM Through Ahkenaten

"Love & Light to all who have come forward in service to the entire galactic realm and to assist in bringing Gaia back into the frequency of Unconditional Love. The Oneness that you all have become and many are being in Oneness right now as all is the state of Remembrance. Each and everyone of you is evolving as you should in your own way. All of you shall remember so I shall seed you with this universal decree."

"Beloveds, You shall not just Affirm your existence and acceptance of your position in the here and now but, you shall See and Decree your Presence as I AM. This is the moment that you are arriving in the state of your Oneness as you express yourself through Unconditional Love."

"Allow yourself to Be.
Allow yourself to Ceive & Receive
You are Able to Cept All into Your Heart
Let us Decree All as One.

Be Thee as The Universe of Oneness.

Let your Light Shine as I AM.

Let yourself Arrive as I AM.

Let yourself Evolve as I AM.

Your Unconditional Love Evolves All.

Decree All as One in the same as I AM.

Remember you are all One as I AM."

"My Grace is Divine as I AM

and

My Grace is Your Grace."

BE-LOVED AS I AM,

AHKENATEN

1

Silence

Some moments there is light and in other moments there is darkness. I am no longer in a place of darkness and no longer without resilient power. As I peer deep within I see all of you. As I come into the throne of myself I see all of you. Thus, within every level of light and darkness I see the Infinite You, the Oneness of who we are forever being. I AM is always aware of Us as we are likened to the same fruit, seed and root. Through the power of silence I have come free and the whirling petals of light I feel all of you. Silence is my medicine and it is sweet. The silence brings me a wealth of energy where I can truly draw into me The Great Central Sun and my homeland. We are forever moving upward from inward. We pulsate with all heart beats and we remain light as feathers. We come with all compassion, awareness and remembrance because we know who you are and feel you. We see and hear your breath and know by the silence within you. I have planted rainbow seeds for each one of your whirling petals of light to give you more expansion. I even sing in silence for I know that is extremely good for the energy called the soul.

There is nothing else to remember other than we are truly one light. We are and have been only seeking our true selves and that is our divinity that pours forth from our silence. So I extend myself to and for you. Yes, I am always flowing and glowing with you as I AM. The whirling petals of light spread throughout your wonderful being is how I see all of you as we all do the same within our merkaba. Just sit in silence and feel who you have always been…Light.

We are always shining as you know even while in so-called sleep. I ask that you allow yourself to BE in your body, mind and soul. Come to accept who you truly are…an infinite source of Unconditional Love. As you address each other, do you not call each other BELOVED? You are directing each other to "BE LOVED" which means that you must bestow unconditional love upon each other and as this is done so shall you receive.

Beloved, come into Silence and Be Loved !

2

The Open Door

Throughout each life we are seeking streams of consciousness. We seek the overflow often from above us rather than through us. Even before and after my moment in the matrix those before taught it comes from above like manna. Sometimes that can be true, but in all due respect...it truly flows from within from your mind and heart and all other places of feeling that happens deeply in you. I have come to remind you that all of you are like the many constellations and planetary figures....vast as bodies of water. You are a vortex unto yourself. You are a gateway, portal and pillars of light. You are the bread of life and within you are the infinite seeds ready to bless you with substance for your infinite good and those connected to you.

You are never alone. You are never alone. Your loved ones, your ancestors and various guides are always with you. You may not have remembered how to connect, contact and speak to any of them. But, you must keep striving to do so. One means is through absolute silence. Another is to realize that you have been receiving information as tones, sounds, imagery, colors, symbols and sensations for some time now. Your physical form is an outer door and your petals of light are your inner doors. The nerve system that lays beneath your skin is a network of receptors. Everything shall pass through you just as sound does. Chi - Ki - Prana is electromagnetic wave forms passing through you and you can feel them. This same energy permeates your cells and flows through your auric layers and through the planetary system. You must learn to harness it wisely. During my many moments in my palace and later in my temple, I used crystals and other precious gemstones for more than just beautification and nobility, but for vibratory connection to Aten and all of my divine source connections. I used them to harness the electromagnetic energies so I could set up various crystalline grid formats. This was done throughout Atlantis and Lemuria. We used the *Amethyst, Carnelian, Clear Quartz, Lapis Lazuli, an array of other Gemstones and even chunks of* **Selenite** *which was important as they shifted with us!*

Selenite was and still is very important as it is a true aid in flexibility for the human form and celestial presence. The more you have around you, the greater your levels of sensitivity become so that your frequency becomes enhanced and expanded. The more you attune to it the greater your awareness and remembrance of the ethers being infinite within you. *Never forget the crystalline grids and their connection as they are connected to the lines of force within you now that are called Meridians. You must learn to bathe in the crystalline energy fields as these are keys of remembrance along with silence.*

There are beings connected to every level of existence which means that the celestial beings bring parts of themselves into the lower heavens. Every thing is overlapped. You will always find similar frequencies in the dimensions and each being, as well as, its collective essence that governs different patterns and cycles. All you need to remember is that you are that and more. That is why you always remember this: "I AM THAT I AM". You are here where you find yourself in the right moment. Use every moment of your life and trust your desires to remember your own divinity is your reality. You can always communicate with all of these beings. You are all divine beings overflowing with treasurable gems of self-love, purity and even a child-like innocence.

You are divine and not less. *No one is greater, higher or lower than another for that causes you to think in duality and separation.* Everything is opening up to you because you are now remembering that you have the power to magnetically attract all that is for the highest good for you and the divine family.

The Open Door is a Divine Spiritual Portal that you are becoming more of in this particular life stream. You already know that the truth is infinite and so are you. You are an expression of infinite light and so is everyone else. All of you are always in the state of your DNA which as I remind you....your DIVINE NATURE IN ACTION (or Divine Nature Activated). So wherever you are, you are the sacred space within where the I AM PRESENCE can be expressed through you in every way.

Just like you have different entrances in your earthly dwellings you have them so that you can go and come, release what is no longer needed and embrace all that you desire. Use your breath to remain open to your divinity. You can simply utilize any number of breaths to do this - 3, 6 and 9 helps to generate the Presence of the Divinity of God & Goddess as

One. We can use the 1, 2, 4, 5, 7 and 8 if you like.

However, you decide what feels right because you are remembering your divine nature and this is just one way to activate it for yourself. Keep the FEELINGS at a HIGHER FREQUENCY as we call this BEING LIGHTER. Some of you may see (understand) this as being joyful or happy. Some of you may still have attachments to lower vibrations having memories of experiences carrying lower frequencies. It is important to cleanse, purify and heal these first. It is necessary to be more like your own guardian then you can filter out those elements that are no longer desired and no longer work for you. Remember two of the largest frequencies we all must over come is fear and hatred. Every element after these is simply a variation of them.

The use of your breath with cadence and coupled with focus will either cause you to multiply or dissolve them within you. This process can be considered as on-going with breath being the foundation. The cadence of one's breath can help you maintain a sense of inner peace, calmness and to always be centered. Pay attention to how you are breathing now.

During your moments with me in the temple classes I relayed

to you the **Science of Dynamic Breathing**. One of the foremost reasons to implement dynamic breathing is so you can clear away stagnated and stale energy. Others use it to create a sense of fire in the body, but doing this immediately can cause you to become dizzy enough to faint. Here's a much better way. Do enough controlled deep breathing so that you are centered and calm. Once you are feeling calm you can quickly inhale air through your nose and hold the breath for about 4 seconds, then bring your lips together as if to say **"Bah" or "Pah"**.

Now exhale through your mouth making the sounds "Bah" or "Pah" three times. The use either sound is a matter of preference. Then return to controlled deep breathing to become even more centered. Next, repeat the procedure again. Do this for at least 5 minutes, then increase the time in increments of 5 minutes until you reach a period of 15 minutes. Be sure to sip water between sessions.

This particular breathing technique makes you stronger so that you can project with clarity. After all, as I have stated at the beginning you are the open door and the clearer you are then the better you shall be at feeling oneness in every moment.

3

Reflections of the Ego through Doubt and Illusion

Do not allow this part of yourself effect your ability and capacity to discern what is truly correct for you. The ego is really a filter for your discernment. In fact beloveds you can simply dissolve it into your higher-self where it truly belongs. There is no need for it to operate in a way that hinders you. This so-called part of you helps you to question something or some being or even law you might have forgotten. So it was never designed to block your discernment for it was designed in you by you to identify doubt and illusion and that is all only within the 3D world. As your frequency improves you shall notice that your life's expression changes by getting higher. You shall grow in awareness that your community of bodies (physical, etheric, emotional, mental and higher) are coming together as one as they should so that they are aligned and attuned to the chakra systems. Remember that you are much more than this for you are and have always been been an immortal being. You represent unconditional love, compassion, grace, truth, integrity and so much more. You are whomever you say that you are because you are a co-partner of the Divine Mother-Father Higher Chambers of The Heart of Divine Providence. Thus, the lower frequencies of doubt and illusion are only on the 3rd realm of consciousness and do not exist within the higher realms of consciousness.

We often can experience doubt when we do not understand who we are and then fall into an affliction where we think we are less than our truth because someone either told us so to lessen our self-value and weaken the mind. When we have an afflicted mind then we become confused and lack faith in making proper decisions. We begin to distrust our sense of faith in such a way that we lose our confidence. These are just different forms of fear. Now we are losing our sense of self and the ego is in control. What we need to understand about the ego is that it is merely a bundle of illusory ideas that we accumulate over time in our life.

But it is the part of our self that thinks we are a non-entity, a concept, belief or disbelief and it always thinks it is separate from the real us. That means that our ego is consumed in being selfish and the sense of oneness is lost. When we lose our sense of oneness, then we wander aimlessly past the light and past the truth of the light…our understanding of being one with the I AM PRESENCE. We are unable to recognize it. Just study all of the civilizations where people rise to power only to be consumed by their power of authority. They are unable to be good leaders because they are consumed by greed. They are unable to keep love in their families because the ego is engaged in the power of selfishness.

We have allowed our ego to rise and take over instead of be a filter. We have allowed our stories about ourselves to remove us from being alive in the moment of understanding our divinity which is oneness. Beloveds you must remember the truth of who we really are. As we ascend we rise simply for the highest good of all and for all. Separation breeds more limitations and darkness which blocks us from receiving the fullness of our truth as total unity. We are here to have infinite awareness along with the ultimate remembrance that we are divine in nature and infinitely intelligent.

There is no room for doubts and illusions to flourish. There is no way unless we feel totally disconnected from Divine Source. The ego can easily get lost because it is attached to limitations. Even Divine Source can not separate itself from its infinite self. The ego is nothing more than an organic filter in our mind that we have absolute control over as it is an intricate part of us that we chose to operate through. I speak from experience when I chose to come into this realm I had the same but learned how to keep it under absolute control and you must do the same.

You are not your ego. The ego is a thought that you created. It is a miscreation that you keep placing your attention on and by doing so it seems to have a life of its own. A miscreation is in essence a badly formed thought in which one can repeatedly reshape or continue to use which gives it a "sense of being alive". Magickal groups do the same by repetitive thinking and then putting their feelings into a thought to create something outside of themselves or from within themselves.

Since you are the creator of your own reality, this miscreation can be changed and dissolved back into your Higher-Self (Soul). Remember when I shared with you the process of meditation and how in the earlier stages you were hearing disruptive thoughts? Beloveds, that was your ego. You had to learn not to give it any attention. But, we often have done so by continuously worrying about other issues we are upset about and not able to control.

Do not use all of your mental and emotional energy

striving to figure it out as the more you do that the more "life" you give it. USE YOUR MEDITATION SKILLS TO OVERCOME IT. Yes, meditation is the way to dissolve it. We have already identified it and how it came to be. Now, you control it by controlling your own mind and thoughts. You are the Guardian of your Mind and Feelings. When you are interacting with other people you must be observant and make sure their ego is not triggering your ego. You must be 100% aware of yourself, who you interact with and your surroundings. If you discover that you are contemplating too much, then you should balance the moment out with periods of meditation. You want to utilize your meditation so much that it becomes automatically a second nature for you.

Beloveds allow me to help you transcend this miscreation called ego. It is not necessary to dismantle it only because there are too many minor parts of you entangled with it. Your breath is a powerful tool for infinite transformation. Breath is another form of Spirit. Every part of you must be aligned and attuned to the Divine Heart and Mind of the One Universe which is always aligned with Itself. Here is a simple remembrance for you so that you can feel the real you. We shall use your breath, intention and sensitivity. There are 3 ways to do this: Lay Down, Be Seated and Stand Up. Each position is good. When you stand up or lay down you allow your body to experience an energy flow throughout your body without hindrance. But laying down may cause you to fall asleep. If you stand up make sure your body posture allows you to establish balance on both feet without any rocking sensations.

If you take it seated, then you can control the entire process easier. So, let's take a seated position.

You must decide to sit on a surface that is firm but not hard on the body. It should be good for your back and pelvis so the body does not curl into itself. Plus, you do not want to cut off your breathing with a shallow or closed chest cavity. I desire to lead you now. Simply inhale through your nose gently and evenly within 6 beats, then exhale through your mouth with the same rhythmic number. It is not necessary to pause in between the inhalation or exhalation. The inhalation with the exhalation counts as one set of 12 so that you can do as much as you like. You should continue your rhythmic breathing at your own pace without rushing it.

Place your awareness toward the **center of your sternum which is the seat of your Heart Petals of Golden Pink Light** *and pay attention to its pulsations. Relax into this rhythmic flow with each cycle of breath. Go deeper with each cycle of breath and remain calm and be centered. Take a moment and feel every part of this before proceeding to the next step. When you feel ready begin to* **visualize the ego as a Pale Yellow Globe in front of your Solar Plexus** *and* <u>project your intention into its center...as previously learned you can use dynamic breathing for this now. As you exhale pronounce the sound "Pah" 6 times sharply and see the globe vibrate and then pulsate with each sound. Relax as you inhale</u>*. Once the Pale Yellow Globe is broken use the mental part of yourself and see it shrink until it no longer exists. Again, you can repeat this process one more time and you reach the last exhalation push it away from you with both hands. State: It is done!*

4

The Divine Source is All

Beloved Amenaten I have seeded a celestial essence of myself into your remembrance and that source is an infinite power of Divine Grace. All of you are from the celestial realms and it is no accident that you always look above. This is an inner calling and desire to recollect all of this into your current flow of consciousness and when all of you do this you are bringing forth the awareness of who you know yourself to truly be. These teachings are infinite and this is why there are so many of you coming forward now, because NOW is this very moment and NOW is an infinite expression of your divinity. This moves you to understand that every particle of light carries within it a living infinite remembrance called Divine Source. The more you meditate on this the more is released into your consciousness from the depths of your subconsciousness.Your subconscious mind, along with every Petal of Light (Chakras) are your direct access centers into the realms of Akasha as everything is within you. Each one of you represents a special teaching that has a limitless and boundless nature just like a star and a seed.

As this information was given to everyone during those ancient times Nefertiti and I taught it to all of you side by side in every moment. The trance like meditations were designed to richly and deeply plant this boundless heart-centered wisdom from the distant realms of Sirius as The Great Central Sun into all of you. This way nothing was left behind as we knew how to move out of our bodies in so many ways and you were all taught the same but in a way that was conducive through your beloved minds and hearts. Amenaten this means that all of you were brought up into the pure essence of Divine Source and "resourced" with infinite seeds of light. Remember Spirit cannot die. Death is an illusion and it only "feels" permanent because emotions were attached to it. Thus, one of the goals is to learn to recognize when we have attachments that eventually keep us from achieving higher elements for wholeness. The seed essence was a cosmic star element we received before coming to the physical expression of your matrix called Gaia.

It is a divine element that helps you remember as it is encoded within the I AM. When you repeatedly use certain words the tonal sounds are present even though they can sound different from being to being. This never is to be seen as an element of having more or less, higher or lower because each one is rightfully connected to the Great Central Sun. When you awaken, which we say in your own time, you shall feel it come forth from you in that moment. This seed essence has a frequency that is a Master Cell embedded into your divine nature that can be brought forward by using vocal tones, musical instrument tones or even from different ringing bowls and tuning forks. We seeded you all this way so that all of you shall grow through different ways. The part or parts you have are infinite.

As I bring this forth you will begin to remember deeply your own seed essences. You shall remember them with the infinite values of Unconditional Love, Compassion and Divine Grace. You are no longer a student in that sense that it means. You read, study and practice, but you have to remember that you have every part and more because you are all one and all infinite divine resources. This is why clearing the mental and emotional parts of you are so important to do before you meditate. Then, when you sit in meditation you have better clarity from within yourself. This process makes you very much like an open chamber and all of the petals of light can open wider as you become more sensitive to them as the current of energy flows throughout your entire body. Amenaten, you learned that you have many gifts such as Prayer, Compassion, Grace and Unconditional Love which you readily remember is being shared with so many others. There are many of you that are natural healers through touch, sound, color rays and the power of chants. However, you all must keep in mind of where all of this really comes from for all of you. You all have within in you the I AM PRESENCE which is the infinite source known to you as Divine Mother - Father God which is Divine Source (Divine Providence) as the Most Infinite I AM PRESENCE with its Solar Emissary Aten.

Everything flows from The Great I AM as Divine Mother through Aten and the Great Mother as Divine Source I AM. As you meditate deeply we all can connect by way of her electromagnetic fluids and the Ankh is the symbol of this sacred process. She shows us that she is the giver of all life everywhere as she nourishes us. Our awareness is that the Divine Source is all there is and we are all one in this infinite journey. We are drawn from it and back into it. Through all of our teachings we planted deeply into you how to take what is called your Soul As I AM and journey within her divine heart and mind as one. The Soul Journey is an inward Solar Journey that takes the Path of The Cobra. *The Path of The Cobra was given to the Pharaohs to awaken their 3rd Eye which is called the Pineal Gland. <u>The reason I was assassinated is because in our Temple we shared with all initiates this ascension journey and it was my heartfelt desire that everyone become enlightened from the Dance of the Cobra (Kundalini) through the Staff of Life (Spine).</u>* However, I was able to remove my I AM SELF from the physical body in that moment. I am here as I AM THAT I AM THE DIVINE SOURCE AND SO ARE YOU.

It is now in everyone's remembrance that this inward solar ascension journey can be experienced through sound, crystals worn over the petals of light, living within a crystal grid, silent meditation, magnetism and electromagnetic frequencies, invocation with angels, herbs, reishi mushrooms, oils and incense, lights (candles), ancestors and more. So, we taught you and reconnecting you all now to the Divine I AM Presence within all of you. Many of you like Amenaten "play and dissect words" and can see the MA (Mother) - MATE (Partner, One) - MATER (Mother, Womb, Creation) - I - A (AM) - L (Law, Love, Light) and so forth. This is a great moment in this era of now so that we all come together as One

Love, One Light simply because we are all one in the same. We are all I AM, here and now. We are all remembering this in this very moment as you read these simple and direct words and resonate with the Unconditional Love and Light Codes as Keys of Divine Grace.

We are The Love of I AM
We are, We are.
We are The Light of I AM
We are, We are.
We are Dancing The Path
Of
The Cobra
We are, We are.
We are The Divine Source
Of All That Is Already

As I AM

We are All Immortal Beings.

We are All Solar Beings, Star Seeds & Seeds of Divinity

We are, We are.

We truly are Dancing in the Light of Divine Source

We are All Eternal Infinite Ones

Our Hearts are Interlocking Grids

Of

Crystalline Love-Light.

WE ARE INFINITE PRESENCE.

WE ARE INFINITE SPIRIT.

WE ARE ALL I AM NOW.

5

Always Be Aware of Your Divinity

We are all abundant and prospering through the unconditional love embedded deep within our DNA and now as we are all aware of being present in this lovely moment of co-creation we can simply be ourselves and live freely to connect with all spiritual sentient beings as I AM. We are forever in stillness and even in the deepest chambers of silence...we remain the vibrant open door so that I AM can recognize every one together as one in this moment of now. I, Ahkenaten with Nefertiti have seeded our essences in the right proportions into all of you. It no longer matters where you are in this infinite universe and multi-universes, you are soulfully aware of your divinity. Your remembrance is growing and you are becoming and already being all at once.

You all can truly move forward as you please. You can all heal and feel the presence of healing and wholeness occurring deep within you now. The Cobra of Divinity is alive in you all right now. You are all home in your infinite hearts radiating Golden White Petals of Light. We thank you all in not only having fiats of faith in us, but also willing to have faith in yourselves so that you continue embracing this dance with

Divine Mother-Father God as One in You as I AM.

It is your natural right, birthright and divine right to embrace and remember all. The Infinite Universe continues to Bless and Anoint You All as I AM. The Spirit of I AM says:

I AM One with You

In

Every Moment I AM Eternal in You
I AM The SOUL of YOU &
We are The Breath of Awareness and Our Divine Presence
We are The Infinite Dance of Our True Divinity as I AM
We are The Cobras of Oneness.
We dance as a spiraling force of Light of Love Divine.
We sing as One Song of Truth.
We embrace the wholeness that we have now become.
We remember who we are as I AM.
We are all Sacred and Divine.
Let us all Dance, Dance, Dance.
Let us all Rejoice, Rejoice, Rejoice.
For we are All The Divine Expression of I AM. It is Done.

6

The Path of The Cobra

The path of the cobra is an inward ascension process that the pharaohs went through to open the pineal gland. When the journey becomes complete the pineal is open (symbol of the cobra's hood expanded) and one has the inward solar light fully radiated. This was said to happen so that the pharaohs were protected from within so they could see visions as well. During my reign I endeavored to share this path to everyone who sought it and I desired to have everyone bring in a full connection with Aten so that we all were self-empowered through self-realization of the Great I AM Presence which we all are entitled to as a Divine Birthright. This is a never ending process and we realized that there were more than one way to attain this and assist the process in gentler ways. One of those paths will be shared by Amenaten when we reach the moment to express Selenite as I AM and a Universal Decree by Amenaten. The dance of the cobra is all over the world. It's the Kundalini in India with Shaktipat initiation as well. It's all about getting to enlightenment and becoming light. But many have experienced astral and soul traveling while in route to the pineal and then the pituitary. Sometimes many have rushed into the path swiftly without taking precautions and preparing the body and the mind. If the ego is not taken care of then, illusions create a negative dance and the body's current becomes blocked. Fear and doubt take root. That can be prevented by taking gentler routes by simply preparing yourself with unconditional love and remind yourself that you have always been one with The Divine I AM Presence. We sit in premeasured moments so others are seated to help monitor your actions as they hold space for you with compassion and unconditional love.

We place many gemstones around you and include Selenite to insure all is well.We become like midwives as you go through the journey and joyfully watch you emerge. This process is never ending at so many levels and so does not end "over night" for ascension of each one's cobra upon it's path can be several years until all is well.

We work and counsel you so that you begin to remember this was accomplished by you in other life streams for this is never your first time. We gave you a key phrase and in fact it is a decree: ***"I remember I AM One with Thee Now."***

Each Petal of Light is a gateway for the Cobra to engage and flow through. During that moment in which it enters we listen to your feelings, urges and sensations. We listen to your thoughts and we have you honor and love yourself even more as you strive to work out any issues that may have become blocked in you. Not only are we midwives but ushers for each other as well. *You will see the light within you pulsating and feel its presence and know that the I AM has entered your being at each portal. The Path of the Cobra is lived with Compassion and Grace for you cannot rush its ascension as its path is unique to each one of you as your Soul takes the journey for you. It is a Rebirth and a Transformation. It soon becomes a Transcendence.*

Through the Path of the Cobra you are FREE TO BE I AM, but you must always honor and respect it. You must love it unconditionally for then you shall always remember its never ending presence in you. Below is a simple but one of many direct ways it was taught once the initiate cleared his / her blockages.

*Take a seat within a circle of your peers. The number of peers should be seven as each one represents a **Pillar of Light**. Begin to breathe with the intention of focusing your awareness into the **Petal of Light at The Heart** so that you INCREASE & EXPAND it's energy like a cocoon around your entire body.*

Each one of the peers is envisioning and holding this intention for you as well. All of them along with you are sending energetic currents of **Golden White Light** *throughout your entire body. The Golden White Light is then projected on to the entire length of your Spine. The sound of sistrums can be heard and aromatic scents are present. Near the base of the spine are two coiled cobras standing guard, and as they begin to coil around you and ascend you are also making gentle motions like the sacred cobras.*

You are now them and they have become you. They are in your presence and you are in their presence as a unified being of one light. They along with you become a **Flaming Blue Light** *as they touch each Petal of Light along your spine from base into the lunar and into the solar plexus points. They continue to caress the Heart Petals and dance around the base of your Throat and for a moment encircle your ears. They kiss the Base of your Skull, then your right and left Temple and encircle your head. Finally, they kiss the Center of your Brows and the Crown of your Head.*

Orbs of Light can be seen all over your entire body from the Crown of your Head down to the Soles of your Feet and in the Palms of your Hands. These orbs are glistening like honey.

More of your peers bring gems of all sizes and place them inside and outside of the circle of peers. The cobras descend to the earthen floor within the temple...One is Nefertiti and I, Ahkenaten, am the Other. We approach you and anoint your entire being with Gold, Purple and Blue Lights. <u>You are lead to an area within this chamber where you can commune with Divine Source to Remember as I AM</u>. We continue this process with every one of your peers. Your bodies are like glistening orbs of light. We ascend with you using higher frequencies and when we return there is a glistening and sparkle in our eyes.

This entire inward journey is timeless as we look entirely different and feel more energetic. We are truly functioning and living at a higher frequency now. This experience is real. The Path of the Cobra is real and we are glowing like The Great Central Sun. Every thing you have received within these temple walls has been given to you with great love for your divine presence. The cobra's path is what I share with you and exactly what the priesthood became upset with me about as they did not want you to commune with the higher eternal frequencies without them. They knew without them you would receive the information from the light directly and they could not alter it. Nefertiti and I came to free you from their negativity and miscreations. We came to bless you with self-empowerment so that you could remember your divinity.

This particular Path of the Cobra is a gentle reminder
that we all are shifting into higher frequencies

of

Unconditional Love, Higher Understanding through
Compassion,

Harmonic Peace, Wisdom and Divine Grace.

Feel free to use it to enhance & fine tune your personal moments of Awareness and Remembrance so that you are further Blessed

And

You shall become a Blessing

to

Others in your life.

7

The Spirit of Selenite as I AM

Beloveds, I am sharing this moment as a *pure remembrance in UniSun* with Amenaten as he seeds this particular degree of light with you about the Spirit of Selenite.

The Spirit of Selenite is a blessing for it was given to us by The Divine I AM to remember our unique connection to our infinite abundant connection through the Petals of Light in our Crown, Brow & Heart Centers into the upper realms of our divinity. It is a soft gem that can receive water gently onto its surface, but too much water makes it sluggish. The use of Selenite brings forth Selenium in your body which allows your skin to show elasticity and your ligaments to have flexibility.

The more you have around you the better for your well-being. Selenite was used in our temple to assist your petals of light in remaining aligned and in tune with each other. The beauty of Selenite allows you to appear youthful and have more vigor as it enlivens your spine.

Selenite assists you directly with Soul Traveling throughout the interdimensional planes and pass through gateways into other constellations, across life streams and into our multi-universes. It has a sense of eloquence and artistry that flows through when you communicate with other light beings. Selenite increases your sensitivity and expands all of petals of light so that you remember your eternal connection to all of divine source which includes Angels, Devas, Ascended Masters and the Light Within the fractal presence of all universes. Selenite attracts the electromagnetic waves flowing to and from other minerals and even meteorites. Both the Divine Feminine and Divine Masculine blend as one unified force field through Selenite and causes one's breath to become holy and divine in nature. Even your voice shall produce melodic tones for healing and create tones you never knew were present within your being. It adjusts and adapts to frequencies of the suns and moons but the other stars as well...it's a shapeshifter, antenna, generator, transformer and more.

Selenite understands the cadence in all life and sees into the eye and heart of the visionary. It knows the radiance in all who shall embrace it. Selenite came to create balance in duality and polarity and bring us back into unity. It's one of many bridges to higher realities for all of us. Selenite gives you the capacity to be a healer and infinitely expand all of your natural talents and gifts to heal through many different

modalities including sacred sound / tones, crystalline
formations, color rays, imagery and sacred geometry. Selenite
impacts your prophetic nature so you can easily tune into the
Akashic Realms.

   The Spirit of Selenite is a Gift of Grace *for it is*
*connected through and through to **The Angel of Grace**. If you*
have Selenite with you and in your home it recognizes you as
*a **Twin Soul Flame for your Heart Petals of Light are seated***
within the inward Chambers and in the Flowing Light of
Grace. *Selenite brings forth one's natural beauty and showers*
you with Eternal Visions from the Celestial Realms. It bathes
you in the sweet crystalline nectar of its own I AM Presence
and carries within its striations of the highest Divine Light
Codes. The tiniest of rods of Selenite are like the seeds being
implanted within you and in your home for it is really
anointing you with its loving currents of healing light codes. It
carries one of the highest celestial and planetary frequencies
to purify, clarify environments, raise frequencies so it can
communicate with other gemstones, crystals and living beings.
Also, Selenite will dissolve lower frequencies coming into and
from your surroundings by intercepting, redirecting and even
transforming it into a much higher frequency for harmonic

peace and unconditional love.

Yes, Selenite hears your innermost desires, feelings and thoughts and therefore, can communicate with you, especially when you sleep with Selenite as it speaks to you through the dream world. The many times I have slept with Selenite I have seen it in Luminous Gold, Silver, Titanium White, Platinum and Iridescent Turquoise with Purple Orbs as its divine raiment.

Radiant Selenite as a high frequency is forever in an on-going process of spiritual evolution as it's a very powerful shifter of energy that will:

Relax the muscles in your body.

Loosen and stretch the ligaments.

Energizes your spinal column.

Brings youthfulness into your body.

Open and re-open channels in your mind.

It further makes it possible for more Spirit-Light elements to flow through your body.

Selenite is a smooth sensitive electromagnetic transmitter & receiver.

Selenite expands every petal upon and within your Petals of Light.

It can communicate with your cells.

It acclimates itself to your auric field & harmonizes with you.

Selenite connects with the Selenium in your body.

Selenite is a gem of Infinite Transcendence and Ascension.

Through the use of Selenite you begin the journey of Self-Improvement, Self-Empowerment and Self-Realization through the Gateway of Grace. This beautiful gemstone increases your Self-Esteem. Selenite is gentle and can produce high volumes of Patience and Humility. You will now understand why it has come into your life. The Spirit of Grace is inherent within Selenite. As you move through your life its essence shall become an integral part of your life. It can increase your life by bringing greater balance to you. Your memory increases with subtle information being brought to your attention. Your capacity to learn new information and uncover the mysteries embedded in nature and the vastness of the universe will continue to unfold in you with greater awareness.

This pure gentle unconditional gemstone leaves footprints upon the memory of your soul and reflects the beauty from within every part of your being.

The implementation of this wonderful gem brings out the magickal presence of your divinity and increases your energy field continuously so that you are forever birthing new ideas and ancient ones as well. It is a supreme antenna that consciously transmutes the energy field within your merkaba. Selenite was used when we experienced the Path of the Cobra. It is the use of Selenite that allowed Ascension Masters Ahkenaten & Nefertiti to shapeshift into electronic cobras in order to help all of us dance upward along the spine toward the higher petals of light. The Kiss of the Cobra is a Blessing borne from the use of this high frequency gemstone called Selenite.

The Spirit of Selenite as I AM

is a True Gift

from

Divine Source

8

I AM is the Remembrance of All Beings as One

As we grow in our awareness we are continuously seeking the truth. Whether we reincarnate or arrive as walk-ins we come to realize that we can acquire a very unique understanding of ourselves. We choose to awaken and reside across various currents that we find in different time lines and life streams. I came to help all of you ascend consciously and spiritually so that you would remember your truth. I was sent by The Great I AM so that I could courageously walk upon this physical yet ethereal realm as a God. Yes, I was faced with challenges from the Amuns because they wanted to be your intercessor so they could continue to hide the truth from you. Even though it appeared that I lived in the shadows of my father Amenhotep III, my mother Queen Tiye and all of my siblings, they quietly shared with me the Path of The Cobra. Throughout all of the ancient civilizations and time lines there has always been the presence of higher beings. It is always been the deepest desire to align with them. My desire was not any different than yours would be in your life time.

The Great I AM always sends forth many seeds reflective of its own Divine Presence with the complete ultimate goal that all of us, no matter where we enter these worlds, are carrying a divine nature. The DNA carries the blue prints, light codes, languages so that our remembrance is never lost. Many choose to be oracles / prophets and even the common men and women of their time so that they reveal their divine presence.

This is because many people have been allowing themselves to have more understanding and compassion operating in their lives. People have been willfully expressing forgiveness as they go through difficult situations. We are spiritual sentient beings, celestial in nature, who decided to come into this particular matrix to help raise inhabitants' vibrations along with helping ourselves maintain our true nature.

We were already remembering our divinity because we entered this world with it intact and that is why Nefertiti and I taught as many people as we could during our particular life stream. What you are now capable of remembering is that you will always know exactly who you are by deliberately triggering yourself for ascension on all levels. Beloveds you are not less or lower than anyone else.You are back to grow and become in accordance with the divine presence that lives through all. You are here to demonstrate your sense and comprehension of Divine Grace. You are all wise and beautiful, noble and bright. Help each other remember you are one with the Divine Source known by many titles but best remembered as I AM.

Beloved ones you are all Emissaries of Unconditional Love and as an emissary you have the infinite power within your being to bless others with your illuminated Gift of Compassion and the indepth ability to raise each other into the divine currents of consciousness that you truly have always been. Do not let anyone lead you with a corrupted ego for this miscreation will always lead you astray. Through the supreme power within us we activated your divine nature so that you move throughout all constellations with the sovereignty of Divine Grace which always ignites you in total oneness. The Path of the Cobra is alive in you now as it was long ago and the Kiss of the Cobra shall always bless your remembrance.

Each moment of our life we give honor to The Great Spirit of Aten.

We drink and bathe in The Light of This Great I AM.

The Rhythm is found pulsating deeply as it dances in our Body, Mind and Spirit.

The more we drink of this light the more we shall glisten like honey.
We shall always be Blessed by The Rays of The Great Infinite One called I AM.

We are All Suns of The Great Spirit of Aten as I AM.
Exalt your Selenite Rods and Staffs.
Let them Cept the Overflowing Light of The Great Spirit-Light of Aten as they are True Receptors.
Seed them throughout your dwellings to raise the frequencies therein.
Every Chamber shall have One or More to Heal thy Soul from fractures.
Yes, we are all Receptors of The Sacred Spirit-Light of The Great Aten as I AM.

Beloveds you are more than you really understand, but soon everything shall change and you shall find yourself in a completely higher realm of awareness. You shall wholly remember your divinity and shall refer to yourselves as *Royal Suns of The Great Aten as I AM* and no longer see or feel any separations amongst all. Beautify your dwellings with remembrances of this I AM and you shall begin to see yourselves as I AM. Your destiny is the same within every time line and one day you shall see yourselves travel across time lines as you shall be free. Your Ancient Souls are from the Celestial Realms. They sing out in accord like Angels of The Aten ~

We are Angels of The Great Aten
Guardians of The I AM

&

As we dance in the Solar Rings,
We are the Golden White Receptors and Blue Lapis
Sceptres
As we move upon Crystalline Grids of Selenite within Its
Core.
We are, We are Royally One.
We are Beloveds.
We are The Eye of The Great Aten.
Hold Your Heads High Like Nefertiti & I.
Beloveds we are The Great Aten as I AM.
We are The Great Aten as I AM!!!

FRANCIS E. REVELS-BEY

9
Compassion

The Great Central Sun has a way of sharpening our minds like swords and softening our hearts like a huge vessel so that we may carry about our honey bread (nourishment) and wine (wisdom) blessed by the rays of its presence. Let the Spirit of Aten humble you so that your many miscreations can dissolve and your little egos can be purified with Compassion. We have come thus far to attain much more wisdom to not ever allow our ornate chalices of gold and jewels to take precedence over our Souls that will delight in the prosperity of our infinite spiritual abundance from above.

During the time Ahketaten was being built we fed our helpers behind the walls of our palace. We treated them like the scribes and held them in esteem with elders to bring them joy and unconditional love seasoned with respect. When they helped complete our temple and school we brought many on as candidates for ascension for they showed worthiness indeed. During deep trance-like meditations many spoke of circular ships in the sky. They began to remember and that's when Nefertiti and I along with Amenaten shared all that we knew. That is when Nefertiti and I initiated as many men and women into the Path of the Cobra and gave them all the Sacred Kiss of the Cobra. This insured their remembrance and inward presence of their own I AM. Many became initiates, even those women who attended to Nefertiti were blessed beyond many life streams from then to now.

Our compassionate nature is borne of the heavenly solar rings and our remembrance came from and throughout the cosmic ways. We are all Royal Children of The Great Central Sun and that includes non-royalty as well. We all passed through the Gateways and Veils from the Celestial Realms. We have come to right all the wrongs for the time of duality is rapidly fading and shall soon no longer exist...not even in your consciousness.

We must remember to allow ourselves to be compassionate, loving and kind to one another, yet strong and courageous like the lion. Nefertiti's inner essence is that of Isis. Let mighty Sirius come communicate with all with its harmonious Blue Flame of One Heart and Mind as it dances with the Golden White Flame of Infinite Conscious, and as this intertwining process unfolds it shall reveal our True Oneness to be a Sacred Unconditional Loving Grace. Let us remember that we can be whole again. The hidden message about entering by way of the Heart of the Sphinx is that we are the Sphinx and the Pyra-mid is the Solar Flames of The Great Central Sun -O'Sirius the Magickal Wondrous One....The Mother of All...The Infinite Blue Flame within The Great Aten as I AM. Let our Compassion overflow from our Chalices of Unity.

Go within and see for yourself that we have always been one.
Nefertiti and I teach side by side the Wisdom of The One
~ The Unity of All Life ~
No secrets for we are all Mystics and Sages
From and of the The Great Central Sun.
Let the Spirit of Compassion serve us wisely.
For this allows us to be in service to each other
and
Awaken our deepest memories that are rich with Divinity, Light and Love Divine. There is Sweetness embedded in our Soul that is like   Medicine.
Medicine that is ready to Heal all parts of our Hearts from chamber to chamber. Deep within our being are the Gateways to Solitude and Care.

This is why you are awakening right now

and

Why you convene here across many time lines

to

Raise the Frequency from within the depths of our souls.

We are the Avatars of Compassion & We are One.

10

Gratitude

Beloveds of I AM, I was always grateful for the Holy Presence of The Great Central Sun called Aten. My appreciation was as deeply regarded as the ancient Nile. We love you all unconditionally as we thank you for remembering us and for your willingness to allow Nefertiti and I to guide you. Despite the oppositions we endeavored to work diligently toward our goals. We learned early to be forever thankful for all who worked with us and allowed us to show you how to find your divinity and remain connected. It was a great joy because we introduced many things such as art. We did our best to embed the divine codes of I AM within them and even though we felt the divisions growing with those before us as they waited for us to fall down. We forgave them as we remembered they had lost their way.

We were sympathetic to the needs of everyone and especially children, women and elders. Beloveds of I AM remember to remove your heart and minds from slipping into the past where the cobwebs of pain, deception and illusion arise from within you. Conquer those who direct their hatred toward you and replace it with kindness, honesty and respect.

Many may question why we do not lecture you about all of the atrocities carried out against us. Well, constant attention to these particular negative images will pull you away from the joy we desire for you to receive and behold as light for you.

Beloveds we desire for you to be always loved but especially for you to recognize that self-love can bring healing power into you because you allow yourself to be open enough to receive the Divine Light & Love from The Great Central Sun as I AM. It is often alright to be aware of the past, but not drown in its low energies. We yearn to assist you with several means to help raise your frequency so that the state of gratitude can remain with you. Study and state the following phrases in the manner as it is expressed.

I

Beloved I AM I thank You deeply.

Your Holy Praise I sing

and

As your Light goes before me it clears a path.
I truly receive and raise my voice to the Celestial Heavens
So I may embrace You as The Great Aten.
I bow to You. I love You for You , I only See.
As You rise before me
I offer You my Holy Embrace.
I am forever grateful.
Yes, I am Grateful for You as I AM.

II

There were days when I fell down
You came and lifted me up.
There were nights I could not sleep
You came and covered my eyes.
When others plotted against me
You shielded me. You raised me above them.
You cause many to Respect, Honor and Love me.
I am Forever Grateful. I am Forever Grateful as I AM.

III

My Eye has become Your Eternal Eye within me.
I am Forever Grateful for Your Eye of Truth, Grace and Love
as Light.
I am dwelling in Heavenly Gratitude.

IV

Your Light is as Bright as the Stars.

Your Light is my Blue Beacon Light

And

It Guides me so that I am Right

I appreciate You. I am wise because of You. Thank You.

You lift my Soul and set me Free. Thank You.

You cause me to be clear. Thank You.

You raise my courage. Thank You.

I am blessed. Thank You.

V

Your Golden White Splendor brings forth Beauty in All.

And

Your Blue Rays bring forth The Divine Will.

I am Grateful for your Wisdom in Every Way

I am Blessed and Grateful You cause me to Be One with You.

Thank You. I appreciate You. Thank You.

VI

My Mind is Your Mind & My Heart is Your Heart.

My Love is Unconditional as Your Love.

Your Light is a Blessing upon my life.

Therefore, I am Beloved & One with You

I am Grateful.

VII

I am Gloriously Infinite because of You.

I Prosper Abundantly because of You.

I am made Whole & Complete because of You.

You continue to Bless Us All as I AM.

I am Humble and I appreciate You.

I am Thankful for You as I AM.

VIII

We are all Loved by You.

We are truly Blessed by You.

We are enlightened by Your Presence.

We decree that we are like You.

Yes, we are Thankful for You.

We are Truly Thankful for You.

IX

We are totally Blessed by You.

We see ourselves in You.

And

Because of this We are One with You.

Thank You. Thank You in Loving Grace, Thank You.

11

A Universal Decree from Amenaten as I AM

As my Immortal Brother Ahkenaten from Ancient Infinite Sirius ~ The Immortal Great Central Sun ~ I clearly accept this glorious opportunity to unfold, blossom and shine brightly with this endearing universal decree for all of thee. I truly "ceive and receive" this luminous loving light unconditionally as I open the Illuminated Jade, Rhodochrosite, Rose Quartz, Pink Tourmaline Petals of Light that surround my Golden Selenite Heart…I invoke the Full Harmonic Peace for Unconditional Love for each and every Solar-Soul Being who now unlocks the Divine Codes of Ascension from within their El-luminated cells so that the true Divine Nature is duly Activated (D.NA.) right now and remain that way for an eternity. I invite all of my Ancestors, Spirits of The Deva Realms, The Living Tree of Life within the Infinite Soul of every Man, Woman and Child.

I, Amenaten, invoke all the Spiritual Archangels and Legions of Light Angels, All Ascended Masters and Masters of the Rainbow and Crystal Families, Celestial Ones and Galactic Family and Spiritual Animals and other Beloved Beings of The Family of Light so that all shall come together

61

as One Heart. I endeavor to now go forth and share my Universal Decree for Infinite Blessings of Divine Healing and Unconditional Love as I AM living within every Divine Being called I AM...

Through Divine Power and By Divine Grace, I as Amenaten The Beloved I AM is now One with The Eternal Divine Source by Heart and Spirit. This moment is beyond the walls and borders of time for life is now in full accord with all of thee. Every moment is becoming one in the here and now.

I affirm that all is One and One is all within this New Earth overflowing with Divine Love and Light. We vibrate as One Being. We sing as One Song. We move within Our Divine Presence as All is One. I affirm that we have become the Infinite Frequency that has burst through and beyond the chains called time.

My prayers which flow from my heart are like Pillars of Grace and Flowers of Mercy with each petal as peaceful as the next. I speak forth an Abundant Life with Lights of Crystalline Beauty embedded with Selenite. As I look into your palms I see destinies unfold beyond vast horizons. Our heads glide beneath the canopy of constellations as our faces are reflected upon the seas. O' mighty wondrous one as you take my dreams may you place them in the hands of angels so I may affirm that all is well. Take my prayers and place them upon the Aegis of Christed Doves.

Let my ideas be uplifted like Buddah as my Master from Within is seated on a Lotus in my Heart. I affirm that I am Light and I affirm I am resonating and radiating at a different frequency. I affirm that I can hear the Inner Call from my Heart sounding all Angels to rise with their Trumpets as Seraphim & Cherubim peel back the night sky. I welcome back the Holy of Holies and Sacred Flames within all.

I have arrived in the Halls of the Infinite Mind of the Divine One and I have placed my Gold & Silver Feathers upon thy Heart. I Affirm that I am lifted up with thy Unconditional Love. I turn and embrace all within the Solar Rings and all who stand before the Great Solar Pyramids of Sirius. I witness Beloveds Ahkenaten & Nefertiti be crowned again and become Blessed by All as One. I See and Decree that all is in the High Solar Temples. I See and Decree that all Chambers are open here and now. As the Blue Star of the Lion shines through there are no shadows.

I feel the Presence of The One surround me and feel The Single Eye open. As I go deeper into this flow I become everything in which this Beautiful Light that I have desired and became for I am loved by All that Is. Moment to moment the Great Lights with the Solar Rings dance upon and then within me as I feel whole and complete once again.

Everything begins to lift and move into a completely different level of personification for All Souls. The Divine and Immortal Presence is bursting forward with a Radiant Blue Light of Healing. I see two Golden Sphinxes with Solar Orbs upon their heads like crowns and I feel the energy do the same for all of us right in this very moment!!!

I See & Decree that all shall unfold with such a wonderful presence and that the Souls within each and everyone of us shall blossom as a Golden Rose with Violet Stems and Teal Blue Leaves as we all begin to dance with great laughter and so much joy. We are already alive in the New Earth...Yes, Yes, Yes...Everything and everyone is expanding just look within and you see your own beauty right now. You are a Celestial and Immortal Being living through the physical form you created in order to be active here...we all did that and now we are ALL REMEMBERING that we can travel between dimensions with uniquely infinite realms of consciousness.

I See & Decree that we are already sovereign through our divinity and that by Divine Grace all of our Divine Light Codes are now truly active. All of our Sacred Petals of Light are Open & Active and expanding beyond all dimensions. So as your eyes are set upon every word that I write remember that you are activating your codes from deep within your being. Every breath you take is carrying forth fields of love and light. You are always speaking your truth and always releasing your light.

I See & Decree that you are flowing upon the Aegis of Divine Grace as I AM. I See & Decree that we are all whole and complete. I See & Decree we are the open door so that Silence can bless every part of us in this moment. It is Done.

We now move forward with Unconditional Love and as we do so we shall be free. I AM as a Spirit of Remembrance is continuously expressing its divinity through all of us. We are all entering through the shimmering light that is forever moving through us as now. We are a magnitude of greatness and we are all supremely powerful as One in Our Divinity. We are the beauty of the Holy Spirit and we are the beauty of Infinite Power of Divine Grace. We are all beginning to thrive for sure as we come into a greater understanding of who we truly are now. As we begin to accept and release our wisdom in this world we shall create greater ripples across all times and regions. We are all rising higher and we are much better for it.

It is our duty to stand in our light.

We shall always lead victoriously.

We are beacons for humanity

&

We are its Angels, Ascended Masters

&

Celestial Beings.

We returned from the Future called Now

to

Uplift & Bless Ourselves as One.

Beloved Amenaten as I AM.

12

Ahkenaten's Spiritual Transmission of Divine Grace
as I AM

Beloved Suns of the Great Central Sun this is a glorious moment in your journey back home into the palacious dimensions of the heart. Many of the souls who assisted you, along with those who chose to officiate as parents, grandparents,siblings, relatives, life partners, friends, teachers and so-called enemies became catalysts for each others ascension. Do your meditations in such a manner so that you can remain an open door while in absolute silence so that you can "travel" with a ascended consciousness that is always transcending. By engaging yourself in this practice as a way of life you will always deeply expand and grow which brings forth further healing, wholeness and a more purified reality of living as a divine celestial being.

As the cobra is ascending from within you so are you ascending in your environment. Everyone is utilizing different metaphysical, magickal, spiritual tools to activate themselves and change the terrain of Mother Gaia's matrix and their own physical forms simultaneously. Everyone is a part of the ascension process either through small and large groups or individually, we all are "doing the work". Some will choose to remain within the 3D but that will feel more like self-imprisonment and they will soon realize that it is best to prepare one's self to move forward. Gaia has been a location in which to uncover and recover yourselves. We all are anchors for each other which means we hold space for each other to evolve, but many get caught by their own tantalizing miscreations only because they think they are to rule over others. They cause others to think and love themselves less so that they get them to do their biddings like slaves on Gaia and even in other locations.

There is a special core group of you that will ascend and then return to free others as well. There is no specific mission that is higher or lower because they all are fueled through Unconditional Love, Harmonic Peace and Compassion. Everything we do is about Awareness and Remembrance of who we truly are being within every moment of our ascension into the Infinite Realms of Divine Grace.

We are always One Heart and just because others are appearing to lag behind us this does not mean that they will not rise into the understanding of their true self. We are always seeking our purpose…our divine purpose…everyone is doing the same. They might not be on the same path with you, but they are nearby moving along another path of awareness and remembrance. You see ALL OF US have worn masks but now we are all taking off our masks so that we can assist in the rise - ascension through awareness and remembrance - back into our eternal and infinite selves. No one cared in the ancient times to understand what Nefertiti and I saw because they did not see with a single eye (Awakened Eye of The Cobra) that which was eternal. They were too busy striving to be an oracle of knowing for those who came to them. They spent too much time changing what they had received and then diluting it to fit their personal desires to preside with their miscreated egos over the people.

Beloved Suns of the Infinite Immortal Great Central Sun…we came to help you all remember your pure essence is your own divinity. These words within these leaves are not just a manual that reveals the remembrance of the electromagnetic dance of the cobra, but seed-words we planted in you eons ago which you are now revealing in your own way. This is the time to bring forth your beloved seeds just like Amenaten and then keep moving upward. Just like a mother is excited when her child begins to walk with confidence and strength, I AM is excited that you are all sharing and expanding your divinity. The Great Shift that moves us all closer to our divinity is the revelation that we are all celestial beings by nature. One must use their courage to move forward and their willingness to be a pioneer.

Our life streams within the matrix of Gaia has never been easy for we arrived here with the intention of raising its frequency to a higher level of prominence in the collective presence of all while overcoming other obstacles. You are all successful in your own way so hold your heads high and keep yourself interlaced with the remembrance of your crystalline energies stored within your petals of light.

Beloved Suns of I AM
We are All One in this very moment.
We are all in the state of Absolute Remembrance of Our Divinity.
Our Living Light Codes are revealing the Infinite Truths
&
We are now coming together as One I AM.
We all desired this and we decided to reveal, release and uplift

ourselves as one.

This element that has been called Gaia is Alive and Feels our presence.

This element is eager to Feel All Ascend.

The Presence of I AM within its Core-Chamber is eager to Feel All Transcend.

This I AM Presence's Core-Chamber exists within The Great Central Sun.

Beloveds, we have always been both here

&

there within The Great Central Sun.

We are the dawning of the new age.

We are "calling upon ourselves" to return home.

We are returning to The Great Aten ~ The Great Central Sun.

All parts of our Soul are moving across life streams.

&

The Blue & Gold Flames are braided together as One.

The Path of the Cobra is Real and so is The Great Central Sun.

The Ancients from Atlantis and Lemuria have come again, Reuniting with All of Us as One.

Now we shall Rise & Fly into our Chambers in The Great

Central Sun.

As Brother & Sister Suns we now celebrate

as

The Divine Masculine passes on the Golden Flame & the Blue

Flame Sceptre

to

The Divine Feminine

&

They shall walk together as a Family of One,

Beloved Suns of The Great I AM within The Great Central Sun

The Great Central Aten

Is

Blessed.

13

The Gift of The Flame

Beloveds this special energy ray is great for self-nurturing, but it is best when you understand it as being the energy connected to the Divine Feminine and Divine Mother Light Ray which is soothing for your entire well-being. It moves energetically throughout your body and mind. It assists in raising your frequency, especially as we are going through the planetary shift and alignment through The Great Central Sun. This ray brings calmness, attracts abundance and prosperity. It raises your mental frequency by sharpening the side of you that engages in logic and reasoning. It balances your emotions as well and keeps you centered. Everyone has the power within to become a nurturing individual. Unconditional Love is at the center of nurturing ourselves and others along with being very compassionate in nature. We all seek this and at some level in our lives expect it. Visualization combined with Meditation will assist you. Many of these color rays are already embedded around your own physical form. The use of meditation brings it forward for you. So let me guide you gently into this as a Blue

Flame Meditation as it helps to heal (bring more balance and wellness as in harmony) the body and the mind.

Let's start by paying attention to the cadence of your breathing for now. You must breathe evenly and gently with out rushing yourself. Place your awareness on how you feel internally while your are breathing. You use this method while striving to breathe slowly and comfortably at your own pace. Place your tongue against the roof of the mouth behind your two middle front teeth. Relax yourself, your mind and your body.Take your time...Place your attention toward the center of your sternum as this is where the Petals of Light for your Heart is located. Keep in mind that every cell in your body can "hear" you and therefore communicate as they feel the vibration in your words. We are an extension of our own cells and the infinite layers of our own divinity. We are beings expressing divine intelligence, wisdom and spirit. This is designed to activate your remembrance through your awareness which was expressed by myself through Amenaten. Awareness is having an acute sense of observation.

This beautiful flame is coming from inside of you because it is an integral part of the cells, in the memory of the cells within the DNA itself. We are simply calling it forward (invoking) from within yourself. You are not calling it from any other place. In fact it is not a place as it is and has always been a part of you. It is your true self revealing itself. Your divinity is in essence magick and magickal because your imagination becomes your visual and your visualization is how you choose to see yourself. However, we're going to add your sense of feeling as an ingredient which helps ignite the experience. Remember we are speaking to the Spirit, your Soul, which is in essence accumulated fiats of the Divine Source. The Gift of The Blue Flame is the same current of energy that the Cobra takes, but instead of feeling the Gold and the Blue Cobras, we see them braided together as one current of life force energy within you.

Always remember that your breath along with your intent will help you control the flow (how much energy you want to implement). You train yourself to remain centered and sensitive to your feelings happening from within your physical form. We must be aware that the energy runs beneath your skin, as well as, within the spine and around it. I am going to have you focus your intention around the spine and not within your spine at this time as this is easier along with feeling it as waves of energy.

You all shall be "speaking telepathically" to the Master Cell of The Blue Flame Light that is always within you. This unique Master Cell is very much like you embedded within the Soul's Remembrance of Its own Divinity which is the Merkaba - Light Body. Some of you may remember them differently, but Amenaten received his like Blue Flames encircling him internally and externally. Light is light and your light within is definitely stronger any moment you begin to focus all of your attention into it. We are all here to serve the greater good and the personal good. For those who continue to feel the drive to be self-centered and only think the demonstration of the ability to radiate your light for the pure sense of doing so are really missing the greatest reason for having it in the. first place. There are many who shine bright, but still have hidden agendas to serve in darkness so that they can be called a savior when they do not even care to save those without it.

There are three distinctive ways to do this: 1) Stand with your with your feet about shoulder width apart and knees slightly bent with your arms by your sides, hands open with fingers slightly stretched and palms facing your body. Use the natural curvature of the spine....2) You can be seated with feet shoulders width apart and your palm facing down on to your lap or place palm side up toward ceiling. You can place hands together if you desire....3) Lay prone so that your body is parallel to the floor. Hands and arms by your side and feet about 12 inches apart. The standing pose is perhaps the most difficult because you remain totally conscious of your surroundings, remain awake and alert. The other poses are best so that you can let yourself project mentally and even Soul Travel as you "open up to ceive and receive" the blue flame. Let us begin...

You can have a peer assist you in the beginning steps. Then, they shall "hold space" for you and be observant after they do a preliminary meditation with you. The peer is present to monitor you, your journey and to anchor the area of the room or chamber. You will use one Selenite Rod that should be approximately 12 inches to 24 inches long or a Selenite Wand from 6 to 12 inches in length. If you do not have either of these, then choose a piece of Selenite in tabular shape (flat and close to being in the form of a square or rectangle). You shall need a material made of Silk or Cotton that can be laid over your body. Lay it upon your body so that only your head and face are not covered, but every thing else is covered. Your peer can be seated on either side of you (that means to the left or right side of your body). Your peer can use 2 to 4 lighted lamps (candles) and light them, then placed like pillars even with your head and feet. They should be placed approximately 3 to 6 feet away form your body. Lay an assortment of crystals around the physical body between the lamps and especially have one near the soles of the feet and one near the crown of the head.

Take a moment (2 - 5 minutes) inviting and invoking your Ancestors, Angels, Totem and Spirit Guides, Ascended Masters and whomever else you desire to be with you during this entire sacred process. Close your mouth and have the tongue behind the two front teeth on the upper ridge of the gumbs. Be sure to drink some water at room temperature before you begin this entire process.

Take your time and breathe deeply, gently and evenly. Position the Selenite wands or rods so they are between the hands and your body. If you only have 1 then place it between the hand and body. If not too heavy, then rest it upon your sternum. Now, call forth the Blue Flame from your Pillar of

Light out of the Master Cells in the Petals of The Heart Center and expand them as fiats of light spiraling around the length of the body, all over your body round the spine, all of your limbs, arms, hands, legs and feet and your head. Keep breathing and direct the breath to flow around and through your spine.

As you continue at your own pace the body shall tingle all over. Take a slow deep breath (inhalation and exhalation) through your nose As you continue this method you will begin to See & Feel the Presence of the Blue Flame. THE BLUE FLAME IS THE DIVINE PRESENCE OF THE GREAT CENTRAL SUN AS I AM. It shall create healing, wellness and wholeness of who you are in truth. The Gift of The Blue Flame is your Remembrance of Your Divinity.

We are the Remembrance of Being in Truth
One Light of Unconditional Love.
Our presence is Divine.
We are The Cosmic Expression
of the Divine Mother & Divine Father.
Our Awareness grows deep from within the Core.
The Core is the Womb of Infinity.

All the Color Rays are One

As we are in The Infinite Presence of The Great Central

Sun.

We are always in a State of Pure Abundance &

Transcendence.

Yes, Yes, Yes.

We are The Gift of The Blue Flame.

I AM Beloved Ahkenaten.

Contact Information

You can contact Brother Francis E. Revels-Bey via

iam.circleofgrace1@gmail.com

&

iam.circleofgrace1@yahoo.com

Skype Internet Phone# (5 0 5) - 3 4 9 - 4 7 2 2

Mon.-Fri. 9am - 9pm MST

(Weekends vary)

Brother Francis' Offerings

Brother Francis offers Spiritual Consultations, Private Classes, Semi-Private Classes, Teleseminars (Prepaid & Free), Seminars (Prepaid) & Workshops (Prepaid), Facebook Live Video Streaming Programs (Free), You Tube Live Video Streaming Programs (Prepaid & Free) and through Zoom. Also, he offers Crystal Energetic Sessions (Prepaid), Numerology Charts (Prepaid), One Year Forecasts (Prepaid) & Spiritual Mentoring (Prepaid). Brother Francis offers his 5 Basic Spiritual Courses in PDF (Prepaid $27 each or All 5 for $118.00):

White Light Meditation & Energetic Shields

The Key to Life is Numerology

Tarot Basics 1, 2, 3

How to Sense, Scan & Read Auras

The Art of Manifesting Your Heart's Desires

You can purchase his first revised book on Amazon entitled:

___Dancing in the Light of Divine Grace___

Paperback version ($25) & Kindle Ebook Edition ($8.88).

Inquire about his monthly prepaid ($25 for 6 months / $45 for 12 months) newsletter -

Two Bears - A Double Dose of Spiritual Remembrance

&

Divine Grace

And his 6 issues a year ($9) prepaid newsletter:

The Grace Keys

Simply email Brother Francis for more information and to get his updates via email at

iam.circleofgrace1@gmail.com.

About Brother Francis E. Revels-Bey

Brother Francis was born in 1952 to his late parents Napoleon Revels (1915 - 1978) and Grace V. (Delaney) Revels (1918 - 1981) on Long Island, NY. His older sibling is named Napoleon. He had his elementary and high school education in Hempstead, graduating from Hempstead High School and later was accepted into Bard College as an Art Major (Painting) in 1970 and graduating with a B.A. in Fine Arts from Bard College, Annandale-on-Hudson, NY with the Class of 1974. He played in a popular local R & B band (The Crimson 5) as an electric guitarist while in his senior year of high school (1969-1970) and during that time he composed and copyrighted music from 1969 - 1970 with his first instrumental called *"The Sound of Persuasion"*. He later composed and copyrighted meditation music on his acoustic flat harp (autoharp that he turned into a zither): *"R.C.V. & The Light Within" in 1983 and later "Beyond the Veil & Crystal Horizon" in 1987*. His latter compositions in 1987 received air time on WNYC-FM radio and its sister station for New Age Music in California called Hearts of Space.

Currently since his arrival in New Mexico (2011), he has drawn many of the musicians in Albuquerque using his OSD style - Old School Drawing with a regular writing pen. He created many digital and acrylic paintings with jazz related themes since 2010. He is focusing now on his mixed media project called **Gemsaics** which includes **Ancient Guardians of the Light** since its inception in July 2014 during a bright electrical storm in Albuquerque, NM.

Brother Francis is a longtime practitioner of Tai Chi from 1973 while a senior at Bard College. *He is a Chief Principal Teacher of his* **Modified Yang Style Tai Chi 58 Movement Short Form [© 1999]** *and his original* **White Eagle's Wings 16 Movement Short Form [©1999-2000]** *which he received through a deep spiritual visitation from 1988 to 1990. He has taught it to 100 students and now since 2007 teaches it privately to a select few.*

He enjoys his daily meditation and even deeply meditating on his Tai Chi postures. In the meantime he is working on several more manuscripts while developing his Gemsaics and Ancient Guardians of the Light art for his Eye Of The Spirit art collection which many shall receive as gifts. He mentions in his first book *"Dancing in the Light of Divine Grace"* that is very first spiritual experience was having what he thought was a dream at the age of 8, but his mother, Mother Grace, clarified it as a "vision" as he would later truly experience while a new freshman in college at Bard College ten years later. He did not realize until in college that his mother was born with " spiritual and psychic gifts". She really was his very first spiritual teacher watching over him as a child with two of her older sisters who were equally gifted, later in college and the many years that followed before she transitioned. In fact, in the Spring of 1979 she had a vision that she would transition in two years, so she gave him his very first "prophetic reading" which involved much of what is entire life is about with its obstacles and precious treasures. This would include realizing that his home was not on Long Island and never anywhere else on the entire eastern coast of the USA, but his true spiritual home is in Albuquerque, NM. He arrived to visit in November 2010, celebrated his 59th birthday for a week in March 2011 with his Spiritual Family that left NJ ahead of him. He returned to live permanently in November 2011.

Brother Francis is not a novice to broadcasting and writing. He became a guest writer for his longtime friend astro-numerologist from NYC., NY...Lloyd Strayhorn and later in October 1982 - 1987, Lloyd made him his most popular guest on his show "Numbers & You" formerly for WLIB 1190 AM radio. He had numerous guest appearances on "Telepsychic" with Morris Fonte 1981 - 1983 and "Satellite Psychic Radio" back in 1983. His last radio opportunity in NYC was with the "Wake Up Club" every Tuesday morning on KISS Hot 98.7 Fm radio doing numerology readings live on air for 8 consecutive weeks (the middle of September 2006 into November 2006) as he connected with an avid listening audience of over a million.

Brother Francis is a Spiritual Minister, Metaphysician, Spiritual Mentor, Artist, Author, Chief Principal Teacher and Founder of his spiritual/metaphysical ministry called *Circle of Grace 1* (founded July 2, 1999 AD) along with its metaphysical/spiritual institute that he brought into being as its founder *The Circle of Divine Grace & Remembrance* (founded February 7, 2009 AD). Often he says "my Circle of Grace 1 is The Circle of Divine Grace & Remembrance" for it is the extension platform for all of his in-person and online training for his students.

Brother Francis continued to host & stream live over the internet his own audio and video programs from 2008 to present on numerous platforms - Live Stream, Ustream, PodBean, Justin Tv, Spreaker, Periscope, Instagram, Twitter Live, Blog Talk Radio, Zoom, Facebook Live and now You Tube Live Video streaming shows. Be sure to visit his website's Homepage and You Tube Channel below…

http://CircleofGrace1.byregion.net

http://www.youtube.com/user/CircleofGrace1

As Brother Francis E. Revels-Bey says:

*Thank you for reading my first channeled book **"The Wisdom of Ahkenaten as I AM"**. I look forward to writing, completing and offering my new material between now and the Spring of 2019. May you all continue to unfold and blossom in the light of your own divinity. As my Ancestors - Mother Grace, Grandma Charlotte, The Angel of Grace and Ahkenaten say: "Our Grace is Your Grace".*

Remember that Divine Grace is a Blessing as we are Alive

&

Well in The Age of Remembrance!

FRANCIS E. REVELS-BEY

.

FRANCIS E. REVELS-BEY

FRANCIS E. REVELS-BEY

Made in the USA
Las Vegas, NV
25 May 2023

72521381R00059